VOGUE KNITTING
SHAWLS

on the go!™

VOGUE KNITTING
SHAWLS

SIXTH&SPRING BOOKS
NEW YORK

SIXTH&SPRING BOOKS
233 Spring Street
New York, New York 10013

Library of Congress Cataloging-in-Publication Data
Library of Congress Control Number: 2005934945

ISBN-10: 1-931543-97-6
ISBN-13: 978-1-931543-97-2

Manufactured in China

1 3 5 7 9 10 8 6 4 2

First Edition, 2006

TABLE OF CONTENTS

18 DIAMOND SHAWL
Indigo diamonds

22 SCALLOP SHAWL
My little peony

26 SELF-STRIPING SHAWL
All the right angles

28 SHETLAND SHAWL
Grapes of wrap

32 FRINGED TRIANGLE SHAWL
Beyond the sea

36 ROSE LACE STOLE
Modern-day heirloom

40 DIAGONAL DROP-STITCH SHAWL
Anne of green cables

44 FLORAL MOHAIR SHAWL
Nomadic chic

48 SHEEP SHAWL
Counting sheep

52 EASY DROP-STITCH SHAWL
The life aquatic

54 REVERSIBLE CABLE SHAWL
Cloudy cables

56 RIBBON WRAP
Mermaid parade

58 SHAWL WITH CABLES
Technicolor dreamcoat

62 TRIANGULAR SHAWL
Easy does it

64 SCALLOP-EDGE WRAP
Tea dance

68 VINE-STITCH WRAP
Mint julep

70 POCKET SHAWL
Pumpkin patch

72 SANTA FE SHAWL
Frill seekers

76 DRAGONFLY SHAWL
Secret garden

INTRODUCTION

Whether you are rocking out at an urban dance club or relaxing at home in the country, you surely would be happy to wrap yourself in a handmade shawl.

Shawls can be trendy and funky, formal and delicate, or casual and cozy. What you make of it is largely dependent on your own personal style and needs. In fact, the shawl may well be a quintessential element of your wardrobe.

In the pages that follow, you will find breathtaking shawl designs by some of the hottest designers around. There are some easy styles for the beginning knitter and crocheter, and more complicated ones for the seasoned artist. Some styles will be perfect for a casual day at home or at the office, and others will accompany you on a fancy night on the town.

So what are you waiting for? Your future as a connoisseur of high fashion awaits. Prepare to wrap yourself in homemade luxury and **KNIT ON THE GO!**

THE BASICS

What is the next step up from the basic scarf? The shawl. It is simply a little bigger and based on a few different shapes: square, rectangle, triangle. Very little, if any, finishing is required. Shawls are also very versatile: You can wear them as outerwear on those cool days, in the office to keep the chill off, or to dress up an evening outfit. We have chosen a variety of styles and skill levels in this book to entice every knitter. And because they are mostly quick and easy to make, they are perfect for gift giving.

SIZING

The shawls in this book are written in one size. If you are not sure if the size given in the pattern will fit you, then look at the "Knitted Measurements" at the beginning of the pattern, cut or fold a piece of fabric to those measurements, try it on, and adjust from there. It is relatively easy to change the measurements. If the style is a simple rectangle or square, add more or less stitches to the cast-on to alter the width (pay attention to the stitch multiple, if necessary), and work fewer or more rows to alter the length. For a triangle shape, it is a more involved process. If the triangle begins at the widest point, you

will have to adjust the cast-on number. First determine the desired width and alter the number of cast-on stitches accordingly. Then decide on the length to the point, calculate the number of rows needed to get to the point and work the decreases evenly over this number of rows. Of course, if the triangle is worked from the point up, you still need to determine the width and length, but reverse the shaping. That is, cast on the same number of stitches as in the original pattern and adjust the increases. Also note that if you adjust any pattern from the original, you may need to alter the yarn amount.

CONSTRUCTION

There is very little to the construction of most shawls, as they are usually worked in one piece with little or no shaping. However, some more complicated patterns have more than one piece, such as the Scallop Shawl on page 22. It is best to use a circular needle for those versions worked horizontally, to easily accommodate the large number of stitches. Some triangle shawls are knit from the neck down, thereby allowing you to try on the piece while knitting and adjust the length to your liking, such as the Fringed Triangle Shawl on page 32.

GAUGE

It is always important to knit a gauge swatch, and it is even more so with garments to ensure proper fit.

Patterns usually state gauge over a 4"/10cm span; however, it's beneficial to make a larger test swatch. This gives you a more precise stitch gauge, a better idea of the appearance and drape of the knitted fabric, and a chance to familiarize yourself with the stitch pattern.

The type of needles used—straight or circular, wood or metal—will influence gauge, so knit your swatch with the needles you plan to use for the project. Measure gauge as illustrated. Try different needle sizes until your sample measures the required number of stitches and rows. *To get fewer stitches to the inch/cm, use larger needles; to get more stitches to the inch/cm, use smaller needles.*

Knitting in the round may tighten the gauge, so if you measured the gauge on a flat swatch, take another gauge reading after you begin knitting. When the piece measures at least 2"/5cm, lay it flat and measure over the stitches in the center of the piece, as the side stitches may be distorted.

It's a good idea to keep your gauge swatch, in order to test blocking and cleaning methods.

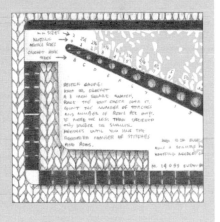

YARN SELECTION

For an exact reproduction of the projects shown in this book, use the yarn listed in the Materials section of the pattern. We've chosen yarns that are readily available in the U.S. and Canada at the time of printing. The Resources list on pages 86 and 87 provides addresses of yarn distributors. Contact them for the name of a retailer in your area.

YARN SUBSTITUTION

You may wish to substitute yarns. Perhaps you view small-scale projects as a chance to incorporate leftovers from your yarn stash, or maybe the yarn specified is not available in your area. You'll need to knit to the given gauge to obtain the knitted measurements with a substitute yarn (see "Gauge," above). Be sure to consider how the fiber content of the substitute yarn will affect the comfort

Categories of yarn, gauge ranges, and recommended needle and hook sizes

Yarn Weight Symbol & Category Names	**1** Super Fine	**2** Fine	**3** Light	**4** Medium	**5** Bulky	**6** Super Bulky
Type of Yarns in Category	Sock, Fingering, Baby	Sport, Baby	DK, Light Worsted	Worsted, Afghan, Aran	Chunky, Craft, Rug	Bulky, Roving
Knit Gauge Range* in Stockinette Stitch to 4 Inches	27–32 sts	23–26 sts	21–24 sts	16–20 sts	12–15 sts	6–11 sts
Recommended Needle in Metric Size Range	2.25–3.25 mm	3.25–3.75 mm	3.75–4.5 mm	4.5–5.5 mm	5.5–8 mm	8 mm and larger
Recommended Needle U.S. Size Range	1 to 3	3 to 5	5 to 7	7 to 9	9 to 11	11 and larger
Crochet Gauge* Ranges in Single Crochet To 4 Inches	21–32 sts	16–20 sts	12–17 sts	11–14 sts	8–11 sts	5–9 sts
Recommended Hook in Metric Size Range	2.25–3.5 mm	3.5–4.5 mm	4.5–5.5 mm	5.5–6.5 mm	6.5–9 mm	9 mm and larger
Recommended Hook U.S. Size Range	B–1 to E–4	E–4 to 7	7 to I–9	I–9 to K–10½	K–10½ to M–13	M–13 and larger

*Guidelines only: The above reflects the most commonly used needle or hook sizes for specific yarn categories.

■□□□

Beginner

Ideal first project.

■■□□

Very Easy Very Vogue

Basic stitches, minimal shaping, simple finishing.

■■■□

Intermediate

For knitters with some experience. More intricate stitches, shaping, and finishing.

■■■■

Experienced

For knitters able to work patterns with complicated shaping and finishing.

and the ease of care of your projects.

To facilitate yarn substitution, *Vogue Knitting* grades yarn by the standard stitch gauge obtained in stockinette stitch. You'll find a grading number in the Materials section of the pattern, immediately fol-lowing the fiber type of the yarn. Look for a substitute yarn that falls into the same category. The suggested needle size and gauge on the yarn label should be comparable to that on the Standard Yarn Weight chart (see page 12).

After you've successfully gauge-swatched a substitute yarn, you'll need to figure out how much of the substitute yarn the project requires. First, find the total length of the original yarn in the pattern (multiply number of balls by yards/meters per ball). Divide this figure by the new yards/meters per ball (listed on the yarn label). Round up to the next whole number. The answer is the number of balls required.

FOLLOWING CHARTS

Charts are a convenient way to follow colorwork, lace, cable, and other stitch patterns at a glance. *Vogue Knitting* stitch charts utilize the universal knitting language of "symbolcraft." When knitting back and forth in rows, read charts from right to left on right side (RS) rows and from left to right on wrong side (WS) rows, repeating any stitch and row repeats as directed in the pattern. When knitting in the round, read charts from right to left on every round. Posting a self-adhesive note under your working row is an easy way to keep track of your place on a chart.

BLOCKING

Blocking is an all-important finishing step in the knitting process. It is the best way to shape pattern pieces and smooth knitted edges in preparation for seaming or for a neat and even edge. If you have no seams and the fabric is already smooth and even, blocking may not be necessary. However, if you do want to block an item that was knit in the round, lay it flat and block the double thickness, being careful not to make creases if using an iron. Most items retain their shape if the blocking stages in the instructions are followed carefully. Choose a blocking method according to the yarn-care label and when in doubt, test-block your gauge swatch.

Wet Block Method

Using rust-proof pins, pin pieces to measurements on a flat surface and lightly dampen using a spray bottle. Allow to dry before removing pins.

Steam Block Method

With WS facing, pin pieces. Steam lightly, holding the iron 2"/5cm above the knitting. Do not press or it will flatten stitches.

FINISHING

After blocking, there is very little, if any, finishing on a shawl. Many times fringe is added onto the ends. You can make the fringe as short or long as you like, depending on preference or amount of leftover yarn. A crocheted edge can also be added to keep the edges from curling.

SEWING

When using a very bulky or highly textured yarn, it is sometimes easier to seam pieces together with a finer, flat yarn. Just be sure that your sewing yarn closely matches the color of the original yarn used in your project.

CARE

Refer to the yarn label for the recommended cleaning method. Many of the projects in the book can be either washed by hand or in the machine on a gentle or wool cycle, in lukewarm water with a mild detergent. Do not agitate or soak for more than ten minutes. Rinse gently with tepid water, then fold in a towel and gently squeeze out the water. Lay flat to dry away from excess heat and light. Check the yarn label for any specific care instructions, such as dry cleaning or tumble drying.

WORKING A YARN OVER

Between two knit stitches: Bring the yarn from the back of the work to the front between the two needles. Knit the next stitch, bringing the yarn to the back over the right-hand needle, as shown.

TASSELS

Cut a piece of cardboard to the desired length of the tassel. Wrap yarn around the cardboard. Knot a piece of yarn tightly around one end, cut as shown, and remove the cardboard. Wrap and tie yarn around the tassel about 1"/2.5cm down from the top to secure the fringe.

FRINGE

Simple fringe: Cut yarn twice desired length, plus extra for knotting. On WS, insert hook from front to back through piece and over folded yarn. Pull yarn through. Draw ends through and tighten. Trim yarn.

Knotted fringe: After working a simple fringe (it should be longer to allow for extra knotting), take one-half of the strands from each fringe and knot them with half the strands from the neighboring fringe.

KNIT-ON CAST-ON

1 Make a slip knot on the left needle. *Insert the right needle knitwise into the stitch on the left needle. Wrap the yarn around the right needle as if to knit.

2 Draw the yarn through the first stitch to make a new stitch, but do not drop the stitch from the left needle.

3 Slip the new stitch to the left needle as shown. Repeat from the * until the required number of stitches is cast on.

CHAIN

1 *Pass the yarn over the hook and catch it with the hook.*

2 *Draw the yarn through the loop on the hook.*

3 *Repeat steps 1 and 2 to make a chain.*

SINGLE CROCHET

1 *Insert the hook through top two loops of a stitch. Pass the yarn over the hook and draw up a loop—two loops on hook.*

2 *Pass the yarn over the hook and draw through both loops on hook.*

3 *Continue in the same way, inserting the hook into each stitch.*

HALF-DOUBLE CROCHET

1 *Pass the yarn over the hook. Insert the hook through the top two loops of a stitch.*

2 *Pass the yarn over the hook and draw up a loop—three loops on hook. Pass the yarn over the hook.*

3 *Draw through all three loops on hook.*

DOUBLE CROCHET

1 *Pass the yarn over the hook. Insert the hook through the top two loops of a stitch.*

2 *Pass the yarn over the hook and draw up a loop—three loops on hook.*

3 *Pass the yarn over the hook and draw it through the first two loops on the hook, pass the yarn over the hook and draw through the remaining two loops. Continue in the same way, inserting the hook into each stitch.*

SLIP STITCH

Insert the crochet hook into a stitch, catch the yarn, and pull up a loop. Draw the loop through the loop on the hook.

Illustrations: Joni Coniglio

KNITTING TERMS AND ABBREVIATIONS

approx approximately

beg begin(ning)

bind off Used to finish an edge and keep stitches from unraveling. Lift the first stitch over the second, the second over the third, etc. (UK: cast off)

cast on A foundation row of stitches placed on the needle in order to begin knitting.

CC contrast color

ch chain(s)

cm centimeter(s)

cn cable needle

cont continu(e)(ing)

dc double crochet (UK: tr—treble)

dec decrease(ing)—Reduce the stitches in a row (knit 2 together).

dpn double pointed needle(s)

foll follow(s)(ing)

g gram(s)

garter stitch Knit every row. Circular knitting: Knit one round, then purl one round.

hdc half-double crochet (UK: htr—half treble)

inc increase(ing)—Add stitches in a row (knit into the front and back of a stitch).

k knit

k2tog knit 2 stitches together

lp(s) loops(s)

LH left-hand

m meter(s)

M1 make one stitch—With the needle tip, lift the strand between last stitch worked and next stitch on the left-hand needle and knit into the back of it. One stitch has been added.

MC main color

mm millimeter(s)

oz ounce(s)

p purl

p2tog purl 2 stitches together

pat pattern

pick up and knit (purl) Knit (or purl) into the loops along an edge.

pm place marker—Place or attach a loop of contrast yarn or purchased stitch marker as indicated.

rem remain(s)(ing)

rep repeat

rev St st reverse Stockinette stitch—Purl right-side rows, knit wrong-side rows. Circular knitting: Purl all rounds. (UK: reverse stocking stitch)

rnd(s) round(s)

RH right-hand

RS right side(s)

sc single crochet (UK: dc—double crochet)

sk skip

SKP Slip 1, knit 1, pass slip stitch over knit 1.

SK2P Slip 1, knit 2 together, pass slip stitch over k2tog.

sl slip—An unworked stitch made by passing a stitch from the left-hand to the right-hand needle as if to purl.

sl st slip stitch (UK: single crochet)

ssk slip, slip, knit—Slip next 2 stitches knitwise, one at a time, to right-hand needle. Insert tip of left-hand needle into fronts of these stitches from left to right. Knit them together. One stitch has been decreased.

st(s) stitch(es)

St st Stockinette stitch—Knit right-side rows, purl wrong-side rows. Circular knitting: Knit all rounds. (UK: stocking stitch)

tbl through back of loop

tog together

tr treble crochet (UK: dtr—double treble)

WS wrong side(s)

w&t wrap and turn

wyif with yarn in front

wyib with yarn in back

work even Continue in pattern without increasing or decreasing. (UK: work straight)

yd yard(s)

yo yarn over—Make a new stitch by wrapping the yarn over the right-hand needle. (UK: yfwd, yon, yrn)

* Repeat directions following * as many times as indicated.

[ ] Repeat directions inside brackets as many times as indicated.

DIAMOND SHAWL
Indigo diamonds

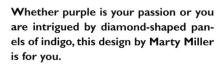

Whether purple is your passion or you are intrigued by diamond-shaped panels of indigo, this design by Marty Miller is for you.

SIZES
Instructions are written for one size.

KNITTED MEASUREMENTS
■ Length from neck to point 16"/40.5cm
■ Circumference around lower edge 56"/142cm

MATERIALS
■ 4 1¾oz/50g balls (each approx 92yd/85m) of Filatura Di Crosa/Tahki•Stacy charles, Inc *127 Print* (wool) in #35 ④
■ One pair each sizes 8 and 10 (5 and 6mm) needles *or size to obtain gauge*

GAUGE
12 sts and 24 rows to 4"/10cm over garter st using smaller needles.
Take time to check gauge.

Note
Shawl is worked from top down.

SHAWL
With larger needles, cast on 130 sts. Change to smaller needles. Work double eyelet rows as foll:
Rows I and 2 Knit.
Row 3 K1, *k2tog, yo; rep from * to last 3 sts, k3.

Rows 4–6 K1, k2tog, yo, k2tog, k to end—127 sts.
Row 7 K1, k2tog, *yo, k2tog; rep from * to last 3 sts, k3—126 sts.
Row 8 K1, k2tog, yo, k1, k2tog, yo, k2tog, k to end—125 sts.
Rep row 8 ten times more—115 sts.

Beg chart
Cont working edge sts every row as established in row 8 of double eyelet rows, AT THE SAME TIME, work in chart as foll:
Note Only odd (RS) rows are shown on chart. K every even (WS) row.
Row I Work 44 sts, beg with row 1, work 27 sts of chart, k to end. Cont in pat as established, working 90 rows of chart and working every WS (even) row as k across all sts—25 sts when chart complete. Work even, cont to work edge sts until 14 sts rem.

Make point
Row I K1, k2tog, yo, k1, k2tog, yo, SK2P, yo, k5—13 sts.
Row 2 K1, k2tog, yo, k1, k2tog, yo, SSK, k4—12 sts.
Row 3 K1, k2tog, yo, k2tog, k to end 11—sts.
Rep row 3 six times more—5 sts.
Next row Knit.
Next row K1, k2tog, k2—4 sts.
Next row K1, k2tog, k1—3 sts.
Next row SK2P, tie off last st.

FINISHING

Block piece to measurements.

TASSELS

(make 3)

Cut 20 12"/30.5cm strands of yarn. Fold in half and tie 1 strand through middle to tie to point of shawl and 1 strand around tassel approx 2"/5cm from top (see photo). Tie one tassel to each point of shawl.

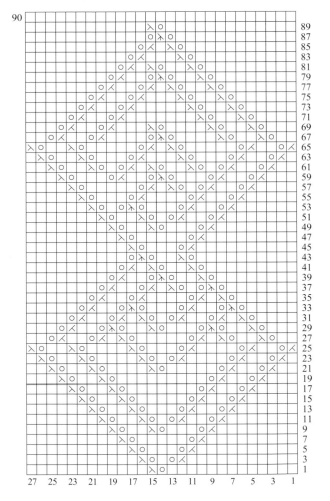

Stitch Key

○ Yarn over

╱ Knit 2 together

╲ SSK

⋏ SK2P

□ Knit

SCALLOP SHAWL

My little peony

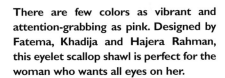

There are few colors as vibrant and attention-grabbing as pink. Designed by Fatema, Khadija and Hajera Rahman, this eyelet scallop shawl is perfect for the woman who wants all eyes on her.

SIZES
Instructions are written for one size.

KNITTED MEASUREMENTS
- Length from neck to point 20"/51cm
- Circumference around lower edge 45"/114cm

MATERIALS
- 3 1¾oz/50g balls (each approx 222yd/203m) of Karabella Yarns *Gossamer* (nylon/mohair/polyester) in #5042 pink with gold (4)
- One pair size 6 (4mm) needles *or size to obtain gauge*
- Size G/6 (4mm) crochet hook
- Stitch markers
- 3 packages Elite Better Beads' Spacers (beads and tubes) item #BB3696-02

GAUGE
20 sts and 28 rows to 4"/10cm over St st using size 6 (4mm) needles.
Take time to check gauge.

SHAWL

FAN
(make 12)
Cast on 3 sts.
Beg fan chart

Work rows 1–64 of fan chart—66 sts. Bind off.

FAN LACE EDGING
Cast on 236 sts.
Beg fan lace edging chart
Row 1 K3, beg with st 1, work 23-st rep 10 times, k3. Cont in pat as established, working 16 rows of chart and working first and last 3 sts every row in garter st. Bind off.

FINISHING
Joining fans
Using placement diagrams as guide, st together both levels of fans. To attach both levels tog, refer to final placement guide and key (the first inverted triangle from both edges of level 2 will be scrunched when attaching to the first level).
Sew lace edging to straight top edge of shawl.

FRINGES
(make 21)
Cut three 6"/15cm strands of yarn. With crochet hook, attach fringe evenly spaced across lower edge of shawl.

INSERTING BEADS
Separate the six strands of each fringe into two 3-strand sections. For each 3-strand section, insert 1 tube spacer, 1 large bead spacer, then another tube spacer. Join the sections by knotting them together below the last tube spacer. Trim all ends.

Placement Diagrams

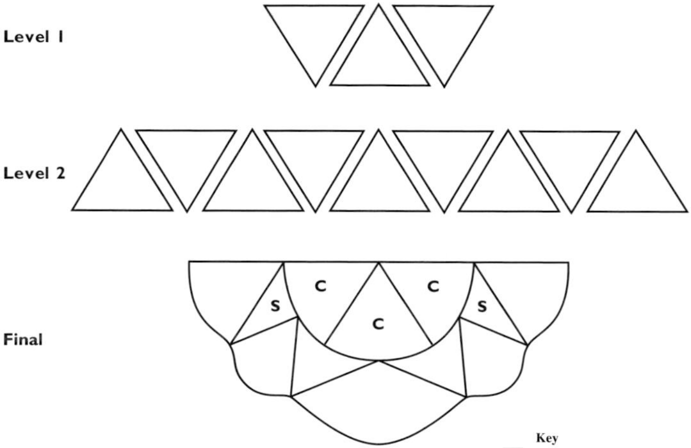

Level I

Level 2

Final

S C   C

C

S   S

Key

S	Scrunch bottom of fan when attaching
C	Center point of fan's base

Fan Lace Edging

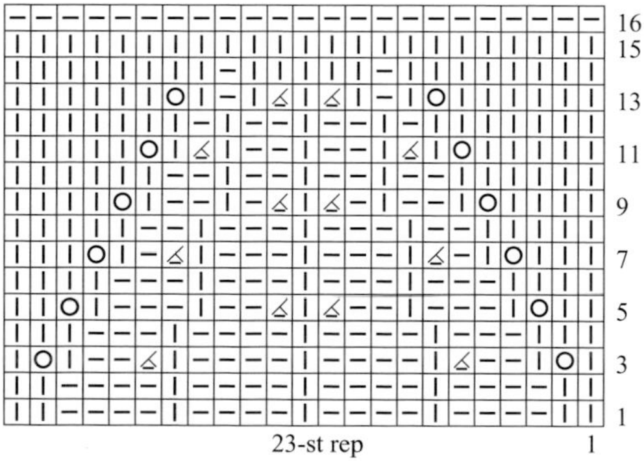

23-st rep

16
15
13
11
9
7
5
3
1

1

Stitch Key

I	Knit on RS, purl on WS
−	Purl on RS, knit on WS
O	Yarn over
♣	P2tog

Fan Chart

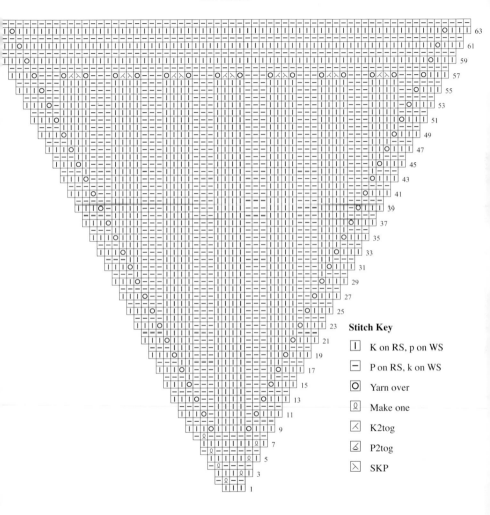

Stitch Key

	K on RS, p on WS
—	P on RS, k on WS
O	Yarn over
Ω	Make one
⋏	K2tog
⩘	P2tog
⋋	SKP

The vespers of color streaming through this shawl designed by Jill Gutman Schoenfuss will remind you of that special sunset you experience once in a lifetime.

SIZES
Instructions are written for one size.

KNITTED MEASUREMENTS
- Length from neck to point 18"/45.5cm
- Length from point to each front edge 40"/101.5cm

MATERIALS
- 1¾oz/50g balls (each approx 101yd/90m) of Artful Yarns/JCA *Broadway* (acrylic/mohair) in #4 **(5)**
- Size 10½ (6.5mm) circular needle, 29" (73.5cm) long *or size to obtain gauge*

GAUGE
13 sts and 16 rows to 4"/10cm over St st using size 10½ needle.
Take time to check gauge.

SEED STITCH
Row 1 (RS) *K1, p1; rep from * to end.
Row 2 K the purl and p the knit sts.
Rep row 2 for seed st.

NOTES
Shawl is worked back and forth in rows on circular needle.

SHAWL
Cast on 130 sts. Working back and forth, work in seed st for 4 rows.
Next row (RS) Work 4 sts in seed st, work in St st to last 4 sts, work in seed st to end. Cont in pat as established until piece measures 17"/43cm from beg, end on a WS row.

Shape shawl at left neck edge
Next row (RS) Work 74 sts in seed st, work 52 sts in St st, work in seed st to end.
Next row Work 4 sts in seed st, work 52 sts in St st, work in seed st to end. Rep last 2 rows once more.
Next row (RS) Bind off 70 sts in seed st, work 4 sts in seed st, work 52 sts in St st, work in seed st to end—60 sts. Cont in pat as established, working left front piece of shawl until piece measures 39"/99cm from cast-on edge. Work in seed st for 4 rows. Bind off all sts in pat.

FINISHING
Block piece to measurements.

■■■◻

In this wrap shawl of delicate purples and grays, Meg Swansen has designed a beautiful twist on the traditional shawl.

SIZES
Instructions are written for one size.

KNITTED MEASUREMENTS
■ Approx 15½" x 86"/39.5cm x 218cm

MATERIALS
■ 3 1¾oz/50g balls (each approx 250 yds/230m) of Schoolhouse Press *Icelandic Laceweight* (wool) in #7208 lilac (MC) ④
■ 1 ball in #1027 silver (CC)
■ Size 9 (5.5mm) circular needle, 24"/60cm long *or size to obtain gauge*

GAUGE
18 sts and 18 rows to 4"/10cm over lace pat using size 9 (5.5mm) needle.
Take time to check gauge.

PROVISIONAL CAST-ON
Leaving tails about 4"/10cm long, tie a length of scrap yarn together with the main yarn in a knot. With your right hand, hold the knot on top of the needle a short distance from the tip, then place your thumb and index finger between the two yarns and hold the long ends with the other fingers. Hold your hand with your palm facing upwards and spread your thumb and index finger apart so that the yarn forms a "V", with the main yarn over your index finger and the scrap yarn over your thumb. Bring the needle up through the scrap-yarn loop on your thumb from front to back. Place the needle over the main yarn on your index finger and then back through the loop on your thumb. Drop the loop off your thumb and, placing your thumb back in the "V" configuration, tighten up the stitch on the needle. Repeat for the desired number of stitches. The main yarn will form the stitches on the needle and the scrap yarn will make the horizontal ridge at the base of the cast-on row. When picking up the stitches along the cast-on edge, carefully cut and pull out the scrap yarn as you place the exposed loops on the needle. Take care to pick up the loops so that they are in the proper direction before you begin knitting.

LACE PATTERN
(multiple of 9 sts plus 7)
Row 1 (RS) K3, k2tog, *yo twice, SK2P; rep from * to last 5 sts, yo twice, k2tog, k3.
Rows 2 and 4 K across and in every double yo work p1 and k1.
Row 3 K6, *k2tog, yo twice, ssk, k5; rep from * to last 6 sts, k6.
Row 5 K5, *k2tog, yo, k2, yo, ssk, k3; rep from * to last 5 sts, k5.
Rows 6 and 8 Knit.
Row 7 K4, *k2tog, yo, k4, yo, ssk, k1; rep

from * to last 4 sts, k4.

Rep rows 1–8 for lace pat.

SHAWL

Using provisional cast-on, with MC cast on 70 sts. K 1 row. Work in lace pat foll written pat or chart 1 until 8 rows of pat have been worked 37 times, then work row 1 once more.

Next row (WS) K1, [K2, k2tog] 9 times, [k3, k2tog] 6 times, k3. Leave rem 55 sts on needle.

BORDER

Note Border is joined to scarf sts on needle at end of every RS row.

With CC, loosely cast on 23 sts. Work in lace border from chart 2, or as foll:

Row 1 (RS) K2, yo, [k2tog, yo] 4 times, k2, SK2P, yo twice, k2, k2tog, yo, k3, k last st tog with first st of shawl sts.

Row 2 K2, k2tog, yo, k4, p1 and k1 into double yo, k12, k2tog, yo.

Row 3 K1 tbl into yo, k1, yo, [k2tog, yo] 4 times, k2, k2tog, k4, k2tog, yo, k3, k last st tog with first st of shawl sts.

Row 4 K2, k2tog, yo, k18, k2tog, yo. **Row 5** K1 tbl into yo, k1, yo, [k2tog, yo] 4 times, k1, SK2P, yo twice, k2tog, yo twice, k2, k2tog, yo, k3, k last st tog with first st of shawl sts.

Row 6 K2, k2tog, yo, k4, [p1 and k1 into double yo, k1] twice, k10, k2tog, yo.

Row 7 K1 tbl into yo, k1, yo, [k2tog, yo] 4 times, k10, k2tog, yo, k3, k last st tog with first st of shawl sts.

Row 8 K2, k2tog, yo, k21, k2tog, yo. **Row 9** K1 tbl into yo, k1, yo, [k2tog, yo] 4 times, k1, [SK2P, yo twice] 2 times, k2tog, yo twice, k2, k2tog, yo, k3, k last st tog with first st of shawl sts.

Row 10 K2, k2tog, yo, k4, [p1 and k1 into double yo, k1] 3 times, k10, k2tog, yo.

Row 11 K1 tbl into yo, k1, yo, [k2tog, yo] 4 times, k13, k2tog, yo, k3, k last st tog with first st of shawl sts.

Row 12 K2, k2tog, yo, k24, k2tog, yo. **Row 13** K1 tbl into yo, k1, yo, [k2tog, yo] 4 times, k1, [SK2P, yo twice] 3 times, k2tog, yo twice, k2, k2tog, yo, k3, k last st tog with first st of shawl sts.

Row 14 K2, k2tog, yo, k4, [p1 and k1 into double yo, k1] 4 times, k10, k2tog, yo.

Row 15 K1 tbl into yo, k1, yo, [k2tog, yo] 4 times, k16, k2tog, yo, k3, k last st tog with first st of shawl sts.

Row 16 K2, k2tog, yo, k27, k2tog, yo— 33 sts.

Row 17 Bind off 10 sts, k until there are 17 sts on RH needle, k2tog, yo, k3, k last st tog with first st of shawl sts—23 sts.

Row 18 K2, k2tog, yo, k17, k2tog, yo.

Rep rows 1–18 five times more. Bind off all sts, working last st of border tog with last st on shawl. Carefully cut waste yarn on cast-on edge and slip sts to needle.

Next row K1, [K2, k2tog] 9 times, [k3,

k2tog] 6 times, k3. Leave rem 55 sts on
needle. Work border on this edge as
before.

FINISHING

Block to measurements.

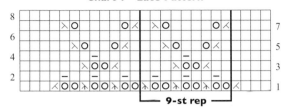

Chart 1—Lace Pattern

9-st rep

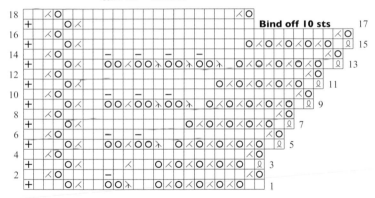

Chart 2—Border

Bind off 10 sts

Stitch Key

☐	K on RS and WS	◲	SSK
−	P on WS	◱	SK2P
O	Yarn over	+	K last st tog w/first shawl st
◲	K2tog	Ω	K tbl into yo

Wrap yourself in a net of moonlight, just like the beautiful sea nymph you are! Norah Gaughan designed this spiraling cascade of gorgeous ribbon.

SIZES

Instructions are written for one size.

KNITTED MEASUREMENTS

- Length from neck to point 32"/81cm
- Circumference around lower edge 60"/152cm

MATERIALS

- 7 1¾oz/50g balls (each approx 120yd/111m) of Berroco *Suede* (nylon) in #3750 light blue (MC) (4)
- 2 1¾oz/50g balls (each approx 119yd/109m) of Berroco *Yoga* (nylon/polyester) in #6401 blue green (A) (4)
- One pair each sizes 10 and 15 (6 and 10mm) needles *or size to obtain gauge*
- Size H/8 (5mm) crochet hook

SEMICIRCLE CENTER

Rows 1 (WS), 4, 7, 10, 13, and 16 *K1, yo twice; rep from * to last st, k1.
Row 2 (RS), 5, 8, 11, 14, and 17 K, dropping all yo's.
Rows 3 and 9 Knit.
Row 6 [K1, k2tog] 18 times—36 sts.
Row 12 [K1, k2tog] 12 times—24 sts.

Row 15 [K1, k2tog] 8 times—18 sts.
Row 18 K2tog across—9 sts.

GAUGE

14 sts and 24 rows to 4"/10cm over garter st using smaller needles and MC.
Take time to check gauge.

SHAWL

With smaller needles and MC, cast on 5 sts.
Row 1 (RS) K2, yo, k to last 2 sts, yo, k2—7 sts.
Row 2 Knit. Rep last 2 rows 65 times more—137 sts.
Shape semicircle neck opening as follows:
Next row (RS) K2, yo, work 52 sts, join a 2nd ball of yarn and bind off center 29 sts, work to last 2 sts, yo, k2. Working both sides at once, cont side edge inc's every RS row, bind off from each neck edge 4 sts once, 3 sts three times, 2 sts three times.

Next (dec) row (RS) Cont incs as established and work to last 3 sts of first side, ssk, k1; on 2nd side, k1, k2tog, work to end. Rep dec row every other row twice, every 4th row 4 times, every 6th row twice. Work even at circle neck opening and cont to inc at side edges until 60 sts on each side of neck edge, end on a RS row. Bind off 60 sts each side.

SEMICIRCLE CENTER

With MC, work 1 row of sc around semi-circle neck opening. With larger needles and A, pick up 54 sts around the sc. Work 18 rows of semicircle center. Break yarn and weave through rem loops. Pull up and secure.

FINISHING

Block piece to measurements.

FRINGE

With A, cut 11"/28cm lengths and place 2 strips each in every other hole of lower edge.

ROSE LACE STOLE
Modern-day heirloom

■■■■▶

Knit in whisper-fine mohair, Shirley Paden's lace stole with open and airy stitches is fine enough to slide through a wedding band.

KNITTED MEASUREMENTS
■ Approx 16" x 65"/40.5cm x 165cm

MATERIALS
■ 4 .88oz/25g balls (each approx 230yds/210m) of Trendsetter Yarns *Super Kid* (mohair/silk) in #1015 grey ④
■ One pair size 6 (4mm) needles *or size to obtain gauge*
■ Size E/4 (3.5mm) crochet hook
■ Small amount of a slippery waste yarn (for cast-on)
■ Stitch holder

GAUGE
21 sts and 29 rows to 4"/10cm over chart pat using size 6 (4mm) needles.
Take time to check gauge.

VANDYKE BORDER
Preparation row (WS) Knit.
Row 1 Wyib sl 1, k2, yo, k2tog, yo twice, k2tog.
Row 2 Yo, k2, p1, k2, yo, k2tog, k1.
Row 3 Wyib sl 1, k2, yo, k2tog, k4.
Row 4 K6, yo, k2tog, k1.
Row 5 Wyib sl 1, k2, yo, k2tog, [yo twice, k2tog] twice.
Row 6 K2, p1, k2, p1, k2, yo, k2tog, k1.
Row 7 Wyib sl 1, k2, yo, k2tog, k6.
Row 8 K8, yo, k2tog, k1.
Row 9 Wyib sl 1, k2, yo, k2tog, [yo twice, k2tog] 3 times.
Row 10 [K2, p1] 3 times, k2, yo, k2tog, k1.
Row 11 Wyib sl 1, k2, yo, k2tog, k9.
Row 12 Bind off 7 sts, k3, yo, k2tog, k1.

SCARF
With crochet hook and waste yarn, ch 86. With one 6 (4mm) needle, pick up and k 1 st in back lp of each ch until there are 84 sts on needle (2 extra chains rem).
Note Chain will be removed after scarf is knit.
P next row on WS.
Beg lace chart
Row 1 (RS) K1 (selvage st), work sts 1–21 of chart once, then work 20-st rep twice, then work sts 42–62 once, k1 (selvage st).
Cont in pat as established, working first and last st in garter st for selvages, until 44 rows of lace chart have been worked 9 times.
Place sts on holder.

BORDER
(make 2)
With size 6 (4mm) needles, cast on 7 sts. Work 12 rows of vandyke border 8 times. Bind off all sts.

FINISHING
Place sts from holder back on needles. With RS facing attach border to shawl as foll:

Using a tapestry needle threaded with a length of mohair, place shawl on a flat surface with needle holding sts in front of border. Working loosely, beg at the right edge, sl one st from the needle onto the tapestry needle and pull the yarn through it. Pass the tapestry needle and yarn up through the first st of the bottom piece (border). Return to the top piece and sl the next st onto the tapestry needle as before, then on the border pass the tapestry needle and yarn up through the space between the first and second st.

Cont attaching the border to the shawl using the alternating grafting method as foll:

On top sl each st from needle, *on bottom*, after the first 2 attachments above, pass the tapestry needle and yarn up through one st twice, then through the space between sts, once.

Rep on the bottom 10 times as foll: *Go under one st, then the space between sts twice, then go under one st twice, then the space between.*

On the last 4 sts before the edge st go under the st, then the space between the sts on each, then go under the left edge st—36 sts picked up in the spaces between sts.

$36 + 48 = 84$ sts picked up in border to match 84 sts on needles.

Stitch Key

⬜ K on RS, p on WS

🔲 YO

🔲 K2tog

🔲 SKP

🔲 SK2P

🔲 K3tog

LACE CHART

39

DIAGONAL DROP-STITCH SHAWL
Anne of green cables

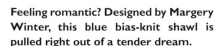

Feeling romantic? Designed by Margery Winter, this blue bias-knit shawl is pulled right out of a tender dream.

SIZES
Instructions are written for one size.

KNITTED MEASUREMENTS
- Approx 23" x 54"/58.5cm x 137cm

MATERIALS
- 11 1¾oz/50g balls (each approx 98yds/90m) of Berroco *Ultra Silk* (silk/rayon/nylon) in #6106 mint (4)
- One pair size 10 (6mm) needles *or size to obtain gauge*
- Cable needle
- Size H/8 (5mm) crochet hook

GAUGE
19 sts and 28 rows to 4"/10cm over St st using size 10 (6mm) needles.
Take time to check gauge.

STITCH GLOSSARY
6 RC
Sl 3 sts to cn and hold to back, k3, k3 from cn.
LT
Knit into the back of 2nd st on needle, leave on LH needle, k into 1st and 2nd sts together, drop off needle.

SHAWL
Cast on 4 sts.
Beg chart-inc slanted edge
Beg with row 1, work 38 rows of chart—40 sts. Cont in pat as established, inc 1 st each side as established until 124 sts (60 inc's total each side), working inc sts in pat.

Straight section
Note Read section before beg to knit. When a purl st is the 2nd to last st on a RS row, drop the st and k last st instead of k2tog at end.
Next row (RS) K1, M1, work in pat to last 2 sts, k2tog. Work 1 row even. Work last 2 rows until 14 LT cables have been worked.

Dec slanted edge
Note Read section before beg to knit. When a purl st is the 2nd st on needle on a RS row, k1, drop the p st instead of ssk; and when a purl st is the 2nd to the last st on RS row, drop the p st, k1 instead of k2tog.
Next row (RS) Ssk, work in pat to last 2 sts, k2tog. Work 1 row even. Work last 2 rows until 4 sts rem.
Bind off, dropping any remaining p sts. Be sure that all p sts are completely unraveled.

FINISHING
Block pieces to measurements. Work 1 row of sc around entire edge of shawl.

Stitch Key

☐ K on RS, p on WS

● P on RS, k on WS

Ⓜ Make one

⋈ LT

6RC

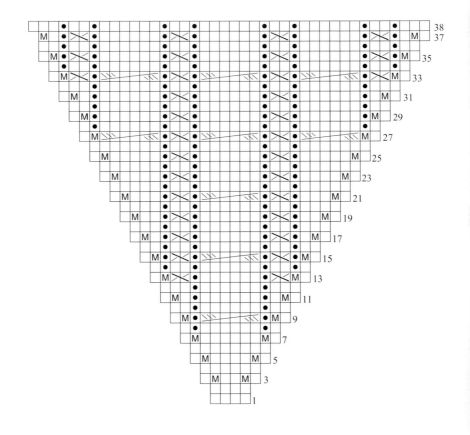

FLORAL MOHAIR SHAWL
Nomadic chic

Sometimes we all could benefit from experiencing the rural side of life—sandy roads and windswept wildflowers. Nicky Epstein has delivered just the ticket to country serenity.

SIZES
Instructions are written for one size.

KNITTED MEASUREMENTS
Approx 22.5" x 72"/57cm x 183cm

MATERIALS
- 12 1¾oz/50g balls (each approx 90yds/82m) of Trendsetter Yarns *Dune* (mohair/ nylon/acrylic) in #80 (MC) **4**
- 1 1¾oz/50g ball (each approx 75yds/69m) each of Trendsetter Yarns *Finesse* (polyamid) in #N261A gold (A), #262 rust (B), and #79 celery (C) **4**
- One pair size 10 (6mm) needles *or size to obtain gauge*
- Size 8 (5mm) dpn
- Stitch markers
- 30 7mm beads
- Scrap yarn

GAUGE
14 sts and 19 rows to 4"/10cm over chart pat using larger needles.
Take time to check gauge.

LOOPY CORDS
Using provisional cast-on (see p. 29), cast on 4 sts. Work cord to desired length. Keep on needle. Work a 2nd cord to desired length and place these sts on same needle as 1st cord. Remove scrap yarn from provisional cast-on of 1st cord and place these 4 sts on needle to left of 2nd cord. Remove waste yarn from provisional cast-on of 2nd cord and place these 4 sts on needle to left of 1st cord. One loopy cord complete. Place on spare needle. Make desired number of loopy cords, placing them on same needle (do not cut yarn on last cord).

SHAWL
(make 2 pieces)
With MC and dpns, cast on 4 sts. Foll loopy cord instructions, work 8 cord lengths, 1 each, as foll: 15", 8", 17", 6", 10", 12", 20", 14"/38, 20.5, 43, 15, 25.5, 30.5, 51, 35.5cm. Change to size 10 (6mm) needles. With RS facing, *k4 cord sts, cast on 1 st; rep from *, end k4—79 sts. Work in St st until piece measures 36"/91.5cm after loops.

Next row (RS) *K4, drop 1 st, cast on 1 st; rep from *, end k4. Leave sts on spare needle. Unravel drop sts to lower edge. Work 2nd piece same as first. Sew pieces together using 3-needle bind-off.

HOOD
Pm 10"/25.5cm each side from seam. With RS facing, MC and size 10 (6mm) needles, pick up 74 sts between markers. Work in St st for 14"/35.5cm.

Next row (RS) *K4, drop 1 st, cast on 1 st; rep from *, end k4. P 1 row.

Next row (RS) K37, turn needles so RS face each other, sew hood together using 3-needle bind-off.

FLOWERS

Note Leave approx 5"–8"/12.5–20.5cm of yarn on cast on and bind-off edges of flowers for fringe.

STARBURST

(make 6 with A and 4 with B)
Cast on 6 sts.

Rows 1–3 Knit.

Row 4 Sl 1, k3, with LH needle lift 2nd, 3rd, and 4th sts over first st, k2—3 sts.

Row 5 Knit.

Row 6 Cast on 3 sts, k to end—6 sts.

Rep rows 1–6 four times more. Bind off. Run threaded tapestry needle through straight edge of piece, pull tightly and secure. Sew final bound-off edge to cast-on edge.

FLOWER CENTER

(make 4 with A and 6 with B)
Place sl knot on LH needle, *cast on 5 sts, bind off 5 sts, sl rem st back on LH needle, do not turn; rep from * 6 times more.

Fasten off. Run threaded tapestry needle through straight edge of piece, pull tightly and secure.

GARTER STITCH LEAF

(with C, make 10)
Cast on 9 sts.

Rows 1, 3 and 5 K3, sl 2tog knitwise, k1, p2sso, k3—7 sts.

Rows 2 and 4 K1, M1, k2, p1, k2, M1, k1—9 sts.

Row 6 K3, p1, k3.

Row 7 K2, sl 2tog knitwise, k1, p2sso, k2—5 sts.

Row 8 K2, p1, k2.

Row 9 K1, sl 2tog knitwise, k1, p2sso, k1—3 sts.

Row 10 K1, p1, k1.

Row 11 Sl 2tog knitwise, k1, p2sso—1 st.
Fasten off.

FINISHING

Place 4 A flower centers into 4 B starburst flowers. With MC, sew flowers together and sew to shawl (see photo for guide).

Place 6 B flower centers into 6 A starburst flowers. With MC, sew flowers together and sew to shawl (see photo for guide).

Sew one leaf to each flower. Sew 3 beads to center of all flowers.

What's more rustic than adorning yourself with lovely livestock? Designed by Amy Bahrt, this shawl will make you feel absolutely country chic.

SIZES
Instructions are written for one size.

KNITTED MEASUREMENTS
■ Approx 18" x 46"/45.5 x 117cm

MATERIALS
■ 6 1¾oz/50g balls (each approx 88yds/80m) of Muench/GGH *Esprit* (nylon) in #27 winter white (A) [5]
■ 2 1¾oz/50g balls (each approx 96yds/88m) of Muench/GGH *Davos* (merino wool/microfiber) in #11 black (B) [4]
■ One pair size 7 (4.5mm) needles *or size to obtain gauge*
■ Size G/6 (4mm) crochet hook
■ 8 four holed, ½"/1cm winter white buttons
■ Scrap sport-weight winter white yarn
■ Black thread
■ 1 button for clasp

GAUGE
18 sts and 32 rows to 4"/10cm over garter st using size 7 (4.5mm) needles.
Take time to check gauge.

NOTE
Shawl is made of 4 scarves, knit separately and sewn together.

SHAWL
SCARF
(make 4)
With B, cast on 10 sts.
Row 1 (RS) Work in garter st, inc 1 st each side every RS row 5 times—20 sts. Work even until piece measures 4½"/12cm. With A only cont in garter st until piece measures 46"/117cm from beg, end with a WS row.

Beg legs
Work 6 sts, join a 2nd ball of A and bind off center 8 sts, work to end. Working both legs at once, work until each leg measures 2½"/6.5cm, end with a WS row. With B only, work 7 rows in garter st on each leg. Bind off.

FINISHING
Ears
(make 8)
With B, cast on 3 sts.
Row 1 (RS) Work in St st, inc 1 st each side every RS row twice—7 sts. Work even for 12 rows.
Next row (RS) Dec 1 st each side every RS row twice—3 sts. Cut yarn and draw through rem sts (to form inner curve of ear). Fold ear and attach to head 1"/2.5cm above face and 2½"/6.5cm apart.

Tail

(make 4)

With crochet hook and A, make a 10-st chain. Fold in half and sew tog down middle, and attach 3½"/9cm from body edge centered above legs.

Attach scarves

With matching sport-weight winter white yarn and using whipstitch, sew scarves tog from top of face to end of body (before legs). With B, attach heads ½"/1cm down face.

With black thread, in X formation, sew buttons on face as shown in photo.

Melissa Matthay designed this deep-blue journey into the wonders of the beautiful sea. It's hard not to feel like you are on the cusp of a wondrous voyage every time you slip it on.

SIZES
Instructions are written for one size.

KNITTED MEASUREMENTS
Approx 60" x 14"/152cm x 35.5cm (excluding fringe)

MATERIALS
■ 100g/145m Colinette *Tagliatelli* (wool/nylon) in neptune ⬛
■ One pair size 11 (8mm) needles *or size to obtain gauge*

GAUGE
9 sts and 14 rows to 4"/10cm over pat st using size 11 (8mm) needles.
Take time to check gauge.

SHAWL
Cast on 43 sts.
Row 1 (RS) Knit.
Row 2 K4, p35, k4. Rep last 2 rows until piece measures 60"/152cm from beg, end with a WS row. Bind off on next row as foll: Bind off 9 sts, *drop next st from needle, pull at each side of dropped st so it ladders all the way down to cast on edge, pull up last loop on the right needle to a length equal to the width of the ladder just formed, bind off, bind off 4 sts; rep from * to last 4 sts, bind off.

FINISHING
Block piece to measurements. Cut 14"/35.5cm long strands to make fringe. Tie in groups of strands as desired to each edge at ladder st.

REVERSIBLE
CABLE SHAWL
Cloudy cables

Everyone needs a little comfort on those cloudy, murky days. Designed by Lily Chin, you can't help but feel warm and fuzzy in this shawl.

SIZES
Instructions are written for one size.

KNITTED MEASUREMENTS
Approx 17" x 64"/43cm x 162.5cm

MATERIALS
■ 7 1¾oz/50g balls (each approx 153yds/140m) of Lily Chin Signature Collection *Tribeca* (wool/mohair/viscose/nylon) in #1283 silver ⑤
■ One pair each sizes 9 and 10½ (5.5 and 6.5mm) needles *or size to obtain gauge*

GAUGE
21 sts and 20 rows to 4"/10cm over st pat using larger needles.
Take time to check gauge.

STITCH PATTERN
Row 1 (RS) Sl 1, k2, *8-st RC, [k1, p1] twice; rep from * to last 3 sts, k3.
Row 2 and all WS rows Sl 1, k2, *k1, p1; rep from * to last 3 sts, k3.
Rows 3, 5, 9 and 11 Sl 1, k2, *p1, k1; rep from * to last 3 sts, k3.
Row 7 Sl 1, k2, *[p1, k1] twice, 8-st LC; rep from * to last 3 sts, k3.

Row 12 Rep row 2.
Rep these 12 rows for st pat.

STITCH GLOSSARY
8-st RC
Sl 4 sts to cn and hold to back, [p1, k1] twice, [p1, k1] twice from cn.
8-st LC
Sl 4 sts to cn and hold to front, [p1, k1] twice, [p1, k1] twice from cn.

SHAWL
With smaller needles, cast on 90 sts.
Row 1 (RS) Sl 1 purlwise, k2, *p1, k1; rep from * to last 3 sts, k3.
Row 2 Sl 1 purlwise, k2, *k1, p1; rep from * to last 3 sts, k3. Rep the last 2 rows until piece measures 1"/2.5cm from beg, end with a WS row. Change to larger needles. Work in st pat until piece measures 63"/160cm, end with a row 1 or 7. Change to smaller needles.
Row 1 (RS) Sl 1 purlwise, k2, *p1, k1; rep from * to last 3 sts, k3.
Row 2 Sl 1 purlwise, k2, *k1, p1; rep from * to last 3 sts, k3. Rep the last 2 rows until piece measures 64"/162.5cm from beg. Bind off tightly.

FINISHING
Block piece to measurements.

Woven in olive and ribbon, this Fayla Reiss original will make you the belle of the ball.

Instructions are written for one size.

KNITTED MEASUREMENTS
- Approx 42" x 42"/106.5cm x 106.5cm

MATERIALS
- 2 .88oz/25g balls (each approx 230yds/210m) of Trendsetter Yarns *Super Kid* (mohair/silk) in #368 olive (A) **(4)**
- 1 3½oz/100g ball (each approx 120yds /110m) of Trendsetter Yarns *Segue* (nylon) in #126 blue/green (B) **(6)**
- Sizes 8 and 10½ (5 and 6.5mm) circular needles, 24"/60cm long or *size to obtain gauge*
- Size F/5 (3.75mm) crochet hook

GAUGE
12 sts and 20 rows to 4"/10cm over rev St st using larger needles.
Take time to check gauge.

Note
Shawl is worked back and forth in rows on circular needles.

SHAWL
With larger needles and B, cast on 120 sts. K 1 row.

BEG STRIPE PAT
Next row (RS) With A, work in rev St st for 10 rows.

Next row (RS) Do not cut A, tie on B, leaving a 12"/30.5cm tail. Work 1 row even in B only. Cut B, leaving a 12"/30.5cm tail. Push sts back to opposite end of needle and pick up A. Rep last 11 rows for stripe pat 6 times more. Work 5 rows A once more.

Next row Bind off 80 sts. Change to smaller needles and complete stripe pat on rem 40 sts. Work 11-row stripe pat 3 times more. Change to larger needles.

Next row Work 4 rows stripe pat, cast on 80 sts. Complete stripe pat on 120 sts. Work 11-row stripe pat 6 times more. Bind off in B.

FINISHING
With crochet hook and B, work one row sc around inside of neck edge. Using photo as guide, use crochet hook to pull up loops, as desired, along rows of B in all stripe pat sections. Secure the long tails around edge by tying A and B together.

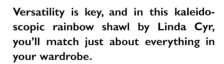

Versatility is key, and in this kaleido-scopic rainbow shawl by Linda Cyr, you'll match just about everything in your wardrobe.

SIZES

Instructions are written for one size.

KNITTED MEASUREMENTS

- Length from neck to point 25"/63.5cm
- Circumference around lower edge 50"/127cm

MATERIALS

- 9 1¾oz/50g balls (each approx 122yds/ 100m) of Noro *Silk Garden* (silk/mohair/ wool) in #87 (**4**)
- Size 7 (4.5mm) circular needle, 24"/ 60cm long *or size to obtain gauge*
- Size 7 (4.5mm) crochet hook
- Cable needle
- Stitch holders

GAUGE

16 sts and 30 rows to 4"/10cm over garter st using size 7 (4.5mm) needle.
Take time to check gauge.

STITCH GLOSSARY

RC (right cable)

Sl 2 sts to cn and hold to *back*, k2, k2 from cn.

MB (make bobble)

With 1 st on RH needle;
Row I Yo, k1, turn.

Rows 2 and 4 K across, turn.
Row 3 [K1, yo] twice, k1, turn.
Rows 5–12 K across, turn.
Row 13 K1, SK2P, k1.
Row 14 K across, turn.
Row 15 SK2P.
Fold bobble in half, sl final st under back of yo st from row 1.

CABLE PATTERN

Row I Sl 1, k to center 4 sts, yo, RC, yo, k to end.
Rows 2 and 4 Sl 1, k to cable, p4, k to end.
Row 3 Sl 1, k to 1 st before cable, p1, k4, p1, k to end.
Rep rows 1–4 for cable pat.

SHAWL

PANEL

(make 5)
Row I Inc 1—2 sts.
Rows 2, 4, 6, 8, and 10 Purl.
Row 3 Inc in both sts across—4 sts.
Rows 5 and 9 Knit.
Row 7 K1, yo, k2, yo, k1—6 sts.
Row II Sl 1, yo, RC, yo, k1—8 sts.
Rows 12 and 14 Sl 1 purlwise, k1, p4, k2.
Row 13 Sl 1, p1, k4, p1, k1.
Row 15 Sl 1, k1, yo, RC, yo, k2—10 sts.
Rows 16 and 18 Sl 1, k2, p4, k3.
Row 17 Sl 1, k1, p1, k4, p1, k2.
Row 19 Work Row 1 of cable pat—12 sts.
Rows 20–42 Work rows 2–4 of cable pat,

then rep rows 1–4 five times more—22 sts.

Row 43 (eyelet row) Sl 1, [yo, k2tog] to cable, yo, RC, [yo, ssk] to last st, yo, k1—24 sts.

Rows 44–74 Work rows 2–4 of cable pat, then rep rows 1–4 seven times more—38 sts.

Row 75 (eyelet row) Same as row 43—40 sts.

Rows 76–114 Work rows 2–4 of cable pat, then rep rows 1–4 nine times more—58 sts.

Row 115 (eyelet row) Same as row 43—60 sts.

Rows 116–160 Work rows 2–4 of cable pat, then rep rows 1–4 six times more, rep rows 1 and 2 once more—82 sts. Place all sts on holder.

FINISHING

Arrange panels side by side. With WS together and crochet hook, sl st panels together, working just inside selvage sl st.

BORDER

With sts on holders, begin working tops of panels as foll:

Row 1 Sl 1 purlwise, *k80 sts from first panel, k2tog (1 st each from 1st and 2nd panels); rep from * across all panels, end k81—406 sts.

Rows 2, 4, 5, 6, and 8 Sl 1, k across.

Row 3 Sl 1, k39, *M1, k2, M1, k79; rep from * 3 times, k40.

Row 7 Sl 1, k40, *M1, k2, M1, k81; rep from * 3 times, k41.

Row 9 Bind off 42 sts, *MB, bind off 84 sts; rep from * 3 times. MB, bind off rem sts, leaving last st on needle.

FRONT EDGE

Working across ends of panels, pick up sts as foll:

Row 1 Pick up and k80 sts across side of 1st panel, 1 st from center of each panel (where panels meet at top), 80 sts across side of last panel.

Rows 2–8 Sl 1, k across.

Bind off all sts.

Pretty in pink doesn't have to mean complicated. This easy triangular shawl by Veronica Manno is beautiful enough for every occasion, and won't stress you out in the knitting process.

SIZES
Instructions are written for one size.

KNITTED MEASUREMENTS
- Length from neck to point approx 29"/73.5cm
- Circumference around upper edge approx 46½"/118cm

MATERIALS
- 4 1¾oz/50g balls (each approx 150yd/138m) of Classic Elite Yarns *Princess* (merino/viscose/cashmere/angora/nylon) in #3419 precious pink (4)
- One pair size 8 (5mm) needles *or size to obtain gauge*

GAUGE
18 sts and 28 rows to 4"/10cm over St st using size 8 (5mm) needles.
Take time to check gauge.

SHAWL
Beg lower point
Cast on 3 sts.
Row 1 (RS) [K1, yo] twice, k1—5 sts.
Row 2 and all WS rows Purl.
Row 3 K2, yo, k1, yo, k2—7 sts.
Row 5 K3, yo, k1, yo, k3—9 sts.
Row 7 K4, yo, work in St st to last 4 sts, yo, k4—11 sts.
Row 8 K4, work in St st to last 4 sts, k4.
Rep rows 7 and 8, working first and last sts in garter st, until 209 sts are on needle. Work 4 rows in garter st. Bind off.

FINISHING
Block piece to measurements.

There's nothing more traditionally elegant than afternoon tea. This adorable wrap by Louisa Harding will be the perfect accessory to your tea and crumpets.

SIZES
Instructions are written for one size.

KNITTED MEASUREMENTS
Approx 43½" x 12½"/110.5cm x 32cm

MATERIALS
■ 5 1¾oz/50g balls (each approx 124yds/113m) of Louisa Harding *Kimono Angora* (angora/wool/nylon) in #5 forties (A)

■ 2 1¾oz/50g balls (each approx 66yds/50m) of Louisa Harding *Sari Ribbon* (angora/wool/nylon) in #1 red (B)

■ One pair size 10 (6mm) needles *or size to obtain gauge*

GAUGE
15 sts and 22 rows to 4"/10cm over St st using size 10 (6mm) needles and 2 strands A held together.
Take time to check gauge.

NOTES
1 Use 2 strands of A held together throughout.
2 When joining B, leave approx 6"/15cm tail at each end for decoration at lower edge of shawl.

SHAWL
With 2 strands B held together, cast on 44 sts. Work 2 rows in garter st. Change to 2 strands A held together and work in st pat as foll:

Beg st pat
Row 1 (RS) With 2 strands A held together, knit.
Row 2 K10, p20, k2, yo, k2tog, k5, yo, k2tog, yo, k3—45 sts.
Row 3 K1, yo, k2tog, k to end.
Row 4 K10, p20, k2, yo, k2tog, k4, yo, [k2tog, yo] twice, k3—46 sts.
Row 5 Rep row 3.
Row 6 K10, p20, k2, yo, k2tog, k3, yo, [k2tog, yo] 3 times, k3—47 sts.
Row 7 Rep row 3.
Row 8 K10, p20, k2, yo, k2tog, k2, yo, [k2tog, yo] 4 times, k3—48 sts.
Row 9 Rep row 3.
Row 10 K10, p20, k2, yo, k2tog, k1, yo, [k2tog, yo] 5 times, k3—49 sts.
Row 11 Rep row 3.
Row 12 K10, p20, k2, yo, k2tog, k1, yo, [k2tog, yo] 5 times, k2tog, k2—48 sts.
Row 13 Rep row 3.
Row 14 K10, p20, k2, yo, k2tog, k2, [k2tog, yo] 4 times, k2tog, k2—47 sts.
Row 15 Rep row 3.
Row 16 K10, p20, k2, yo, k2tog, k3, [k2tog, yo] 3 times, k2tog, k2—46 sts.
Row 17 Rep row 3.
Row 18 K10, p20, k2, yo, k2tog, k4, [k2tog, yo] twice, k2tog, k2—45 sts.

Row 19 Rep row 3.

Row 20 K10, p20, k2, yo, k2tog, k5, k2tog, yo, k2tog, k2—44 sts.

Row 21 Change to single strand of B. Knit.

Row 22 Knit.

Rep the last 22 rows 10 times more. With B, k 1 row. Bind off knitwise with B.

SHOULDER EDGING

With RS facing and 2 strands B held tog, pick up and k125 sts along top edge of shawl.

Next row (WS) Knit.

Next (dec) row (RS) K12, [k2tog, k9] 9 times, k2tog, k12—115 sts. Bind off knitwise.

FINISHING

Block piece to measurements.

Shoulder ties

Cut two 40"/101.5cm lengths of B, double and attach folded ends at front edges.

Finish all ends of B at lower edge by securing with a knot at base of shawl. Trim ends at a slanted angle to prevent fraying.

The images of a beautiful spring day: key lime pie...a slushy lime rickey... and this shawl, designed by Veronica Manno.

SIZES

Instructions are written for one size.

KNITTED MEASUREMENTS

- Approx 21½ x 55"/54.5cm x 139.5cm

MATERIALS

- 5 1¾oz/50g balls (each approx 116yds/105m) of Skacel Collection *Samoa* (cotton) in #87 light green
- One pair size 9 (5.5mm) needles *or size to obtain gauge*

GAUGE

14 sts and 18 rows to 4"/10cm over st pat using size 9 (5.5mm) needles.
Take time to check gauge.

STITCH PATTERN

(multiple of 11 sts plus 1)
Row 1 and all WS rows Purl.
Row 2 K1, *k2tog, k4, [yo, k1] twice, ssk, k1; rep from * to end.
Row 4 K1, *k2tog, k3, yo, k1, yo, k2, ssk, k1; rep from * to end.

Row 6 K1, *k2tog, k2, yo, k1, yo, k3, ssk, k1; rep from * to end.
Row 8 K1, *k2tog, [k1, yo] twice, k4, ssk, k1; rep from * to end.
Row 10 K1, *k2tog, yo, k1, yo, k5, ssk, k1; rep from * to end.
Row 12 Rep row 8.
Row 14 Rep row 6.
Row 16 Rep row 4.
Row 18 Rep row 2.
Row 20 K1, *k2tog, k5, yo, k1, yo, ssk, k1; rep from * to end.
Rep rows 1–20 for st pat.

WRAP

Cast on 75 sts. Work 4 rows in garter st.
Beg st pat
Row 1 (WS) K4, work row 1 of st pat, k4. Cont in pat as established, working rows 1–20 and keeping first and last 4 sts each side in garter st until piece measures 54"/137cm. Work 4 rows in garter st. Bind off.

FINISHING

Block pieces to measurements.

Quintessential to the fall season are pumpkins—and this ribbed pocket shawl by Elena Malo is the ideal complement. Sit down with a good book and a slice of pumpkin pie.

SIZES
Instructions are written for one size.

KNITTED MEASUREMENTS
■ Approx 11½" x 65"/29cm x 165cm

MATERIALS
■ 7 3½oz/100g balls (each approx 109yd/100m) of Colinette *Zanziba* (viscose) in lichen ⬤
■ One pair each sizes 10 and 10½ (6 and 6.5mm) needles *or size to obtain gauge*

GAUGE
20 sts and 20 rows to 4"/10cm over rib pat using larger needles.
Take time to check gauge.

RIB PATTERN
Row 1 (RS) K4, *p1, k3; rep from * to last 2 sts, p1, k1.
Row 2 *K3, p1; rep from * to last 2 sts, k2.
Rep these 2 rows for rib pat.

SHAWL
With larger needles, cast on 58 sts. Work in rib pat until piece measures 65"/165cm, end with a RS row. Bind off in rib pat on WS.

POCKET 1
With larger needles, cast on 34 sts. Work in rib pat until piece measures 7"/18cm, end with a WS row. Change to smaller needles.
Next row (RS) *K2, p2tog; rep from * to last 2 sts, k2—26 sts. Work in garter st for 1"/2.5cm, end with a WS row. Bind off.

POCKET 2
With smaller needles, cast on 26 sts. Work in garter st for 1"/2.5cm, end with a WS row. Change to larger needles.
Next row (RS) K2, inc 1 st in next k st, *p1, k1, inc 1 st in next k st; rep from * to end—34 sts. Work in rib pat until piece measures same as pocket 1. Bind off in rib.

FINISHING
Center and sew pocket 1 2½"/6.5cm from cast on edge, making sure to match rib pat. Center and sew pocket 2 2½"/6.5cm from bind off edge, making sure to match rib pat.

Embrace your inner flamenco dancer in this crocheted ruffle-mesh shawl by Valentina Devine. Bold and thrilling, it will keep you cozy in ultimate style.

KNITTED MEASUREMENTS

Approx 18"/46cm wide x 78"/198cm long

MATERIALS

■ 5 1¾oz/50g balls of Brown Sheep Company's *Cotton Fine*, in #005 cavern (MC) (2)

■ 1 ball each in #310 wild orange, #201 barn red, #345 gold dust, #475 olivette, #520 Caribbean sea, #710 prosperous plum (2)

■ Size E/4 (3.5mm) crochet hook *or size to obtain gauge*

GAUGE

9 ch-2 sps and 9 dc rows to 4"/10cm. *Take time to check gauge.*

SHAWL

With size E/4 (3.5mm) crochet hook and MC, ch 137.

Row 1 Dc in 8th ch from hook, *ch 2, skip 2 ch, dc in next ch; rep from * across—44 sps. Ch 4, turn.

Row 2 Skip first sp, dc in next dc, *ch 2, skip 2 ch, dc in next dc; rep from * across. Ch 4, turn. Rep row 2 until piece measures approx 78"/198cm, or to desired length. Ch 1 to turn at end of last row.

Edging

Sc in first dc, work 2 sc in each sp across, end sc in turning ch—90 sc; do not turn; working along long edge of shawl, *2 sc in next sp, (sc, 4dc) in next sp; rep from * to next short edge of shawl, work 90 sc across across short edge as before; work rem long edge as before.

3-RUFFLE BORDER

Note Use a different contrast color for each ruffle.

First ruffle

Row 1 (RS) Join desired color in first sc at either short edge of shawl, ch 3, dc in same sc, work 2 dc in each sc across—180 dc. Ch 3, turn.

Row 2 (WS) Dc in each dc across. Ch 3, turn.

Row 3 Dc in first dc, work 2 dc in each dc across—360 dc. Ch 3, turn.

Row 4 Work as for row 2. Fasten off.

Second Ruffle

Being sure to work ruffle in same direction as first ruffle, join next contrast color in first sp of 3rd row from short edge, ch

3, work 5 dc in same sp, work 4 dc in each sp to last sp, work 6 dc in last sp—180 dc. Ch 3, turn.

Work rows 2–4 as for first ruffle.

Third Ruffle

With next contrast color, work as for second ruffle in sps of 7th row from short edge. With 3 rem colors, complete 3-ruffle border on opposite short edge of shawl to correspond.

NE SHAWL
DRAGONFLY SHAWL

DRAGONFLY SHAWL
Secret garden

Pam Allen captures the magic of a summer evening. This shawl, scattered with intarsia or duplicate-stitch dragonflies and flowering vines, is trimmed with a knitted lace border.

- Approx 75" x 36"/190.5cm x 91.5cm (including border)

- 8 .88oz/25g balls (each approx 108yds/98m) of Tahki•Stacy Charles, Inc./Tahki Yarns *Jolie* (french angora/merino wool) in #5017 (MC) ■4■
- 2 1¾oz/50g balls (each approx 92yd/84m) of Tahki•Stacy Charles, Inc./Tahki Yarns *New Tweed* (wool/viscose/silk) in #33 (A) ■4■
- 1 ball each in #41 (B), #43 (C), and #35 (D)
- One size 8 (5mm) circular needle *or size to obtain gauge*
- Size E/4 (3.5mm) crochet hook

18 sts and 24 rows to 4"/10cm over St st using size 8 (5mm) needles.
Take time to check gauge.

Notes 1 Shawl is worked back and forth on a circular needle to accommodate the large number of sts. **2** The shaping of the shawl is shown on the placement diagram. The placement of the various charts are also shown on this diagram. The individual charts are drawn separately for easy reading. **3** Chart 1 is knit in. Dragonfly and vines (charts 2, 3, and 4) are worked in duplicate st after piece is complete.

With MC, cast on 18 sts.
Row 1 (RS) Knit.
Row 2 Cast on 3 sts, p to end.
Cont in St st, casting on 3 sts at beg of next 5 rows—36 sts.
Next (inc) row (WS) Inc 1 st in first st, work to last st, inc 1 st in last st. Cont in St st, inc 1 st each side *every* row until there are 50 sts.

Beg chart 1

Row 15 (RS) Work inc, then counting inc st, beg with st 14 and work row 1 of chart 1 through st 65—52 sts. Cont in pat as established (working inc sts into chart), through row 42 of chart. Cont to inc 1 st each side *every* row until there are 92 sts, then work inc every RS row until there are 318 sts, then work 4 rows even, AT SAME TIME, work reps of chart 1 as shown on placement diagram. Bind off.

Block piece to measurements. Work charts 2, 3 and 4 in duplicate st and French knots, reversing and turning charts as shown in photo or as desired.
Note Colors of dragonfly vary. See photo for color or work as desired.
Work satin st embroidery on dragonflies

and leaves as shown.

Edging

With MC, cast on 10 sts.

Row 1 (RS) P3, yo, p7.

Row 2 P7, yo, p4.

Row 3 P3, yo, k2tog, yo, p7.

Row 4 P7, yo, k2tog, yo, p4.

Row 5 P3, [yo, k2tog] twice, yo, p7.

Row 6 P7, [yo, k2tog] twice, yo, p4.

Row 7 P3, [yo, k2tog] 3 times, yo, p7.

Row 8 Bind off 7 purlwise, p to end.

Rep rows 1–8 until straight edge fits along sides on shawl. Bind off and sew in place.

CHART I

80   65

Color Key

▦ Taupe (MC)	●	French knot with purple (C)	
☐ Oatmeal (A)	■	Gold (D)	
■ Teal (B)	/	Stem st	
■ Purple (C)			

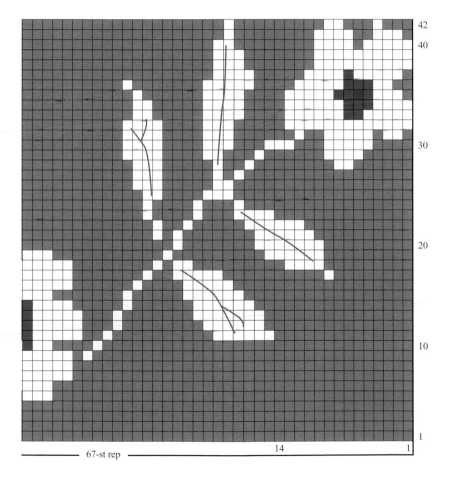

67-st rep

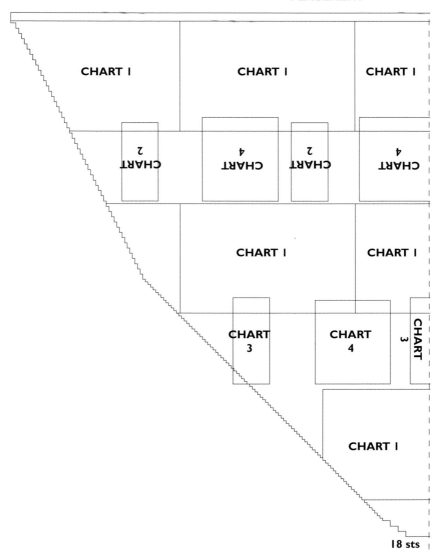

18 sts

DIAGRAM

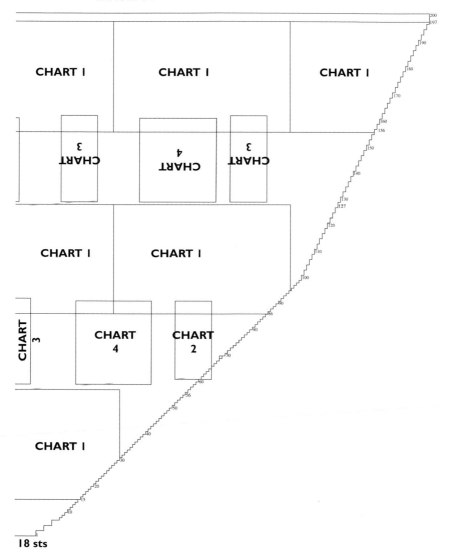

CHART 1

CHART 1

CHART 1

CHART 3

CHART 4

CHART 3

CHART 1

CHART 1

CHART 3

CHART 4

CHART 2

CHART 1

18 sts

200
197
190
180
170
160
156
150
140
130
127
120
110
100
90
86
80
70
60
56
50
40
30
20
15
10

CHART 2

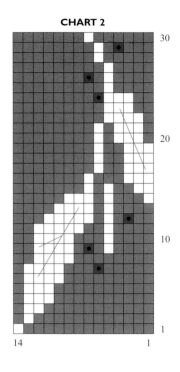

30

20

10

1

14   1

CHART 3

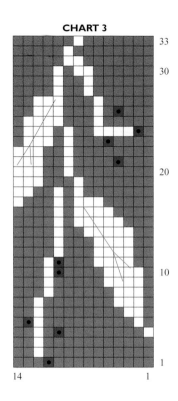

33

30

20

10

1

14   1

Color Key

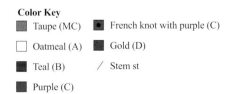

Taupe (MC)　　● French knot with purple (C)

☐ Oatmeal (A)　　■ Gold (D)

■ Teal (B)　　　／ Stem st

■ Purple (C)

CHART 4

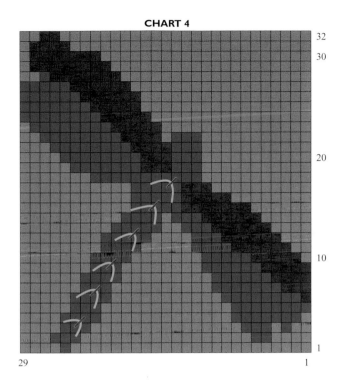

32
30

20

10

1

29   1

RESOURCES

US RESOURCES

Write to the yarn companies listed below for purchasing and mail-order information.

ARTFUL YARNS
Distributed by
JCA

BERROCO, INC.
P.O. Box 367
14 Elmdale Road
Uxbridge, MA 01569
www.berroco.com

BROWN SHEEP COMPANY, INC.
100662 Country Road 16
Mitchell, NE 69357
www.brownsheep.com

CLASSIC ELITE YARNS
122 Western Avenue
Lowell, MA 01851
www.classiceliteyarns.com

COLINETTE
USA Distributed by
Unique Kolours
www.colinette.com

FILATURA DI CROSA
Distributed by
Tahki•Stacy Charles, Inc.

JCA
35 Scales Lane
Townsend, MA 01469
www.jcacrafts.com

KARABELLA YARNS
1201 Broadway
New York, NY 10001
www.karabellayarns.com

KNITTING FEVER (KFI)
PO Box 336
315 Bayview Avenue
Amityville, New York 11701
www.knittingfever.com

LILY CHIN YARN
Distributed by
CNS Yarns

LOUISA HARDING YARNS
Distributed by
Knitting Fever

MUENCH YARNS
1323 Scott Street
Petaluma, CA 94954
www.muenchyarns.com

NORO YARN
Distributed by
Knitting Fever

SCHOOLHOUSE PRESS
6899 Cary Bluff
Pittsville, WI 54466
www.schoolhousepress.com

SKACEL COLLECTION
P.O. Box 88110
Seattle, WA 98138
www.skacelknitting.com

TAHKI•STACY CHARLES, INC.
70-30 80th Street
Building #36
Ridgewood, NY 11385
www.tahkistacycharles.com

TAHKI YARNS
distributed by
Tahki•Stacy Charles, Inc.

TRENDSETTER YARNS
16745 Saticoy Street
Suite 104
Van Nuys, CA 91406
www.trendsetteryarns.com

UNIQUE KOLOURS
28 N. Bacton Hill Rd
Malvern, PA 19355
www.uniquekolours.com

CANADIAN RESOURCES

Write to US resources for mail-order availability of yarns not listed.

CNS YARNS
5333 Casgrain Avenue,
Suite 1204
Montreal Quebec
Canada - H2T 1X3
www.cnsyarns.com

DIAMOND YARNS
155 Martin Ross, Unit 3,
Toronto, Ontario, M3J 2L9
Canada
www.diamondyarn.com

UK RESOURCES

Not all yarns used in this book are available in the UK. For yarns not available, make a comparable substitute or contact the US manufacturer for purchasing and mail-order information.

COLINETTE
Llanfair Caereinion,
Powy, Wales, SY21 0SG
United Kingdom
www.colinette.com

VOGUE KNITTING SHAWLS

Editorial Director
TRISHA MALCOLM

Yarn Editor
TANIS GRAY

Art Director
CHI LING MOY

Technical Illustrations
ULI MONCH

Executive Editor
CARLA S. SCOTT

Production Manager
DAVID JOINNIDES

Book Division Manager
ERICA SMITH

Photography
JACK DEUTSCH STUDIOS

Graphic Designer
SHEENA T. PAUL

Stylist
LAURA MAFFEO

Instructions Editor
KAREN GREENWALD

■

President, Sixth&Spring Books
ART JOINNIDES

LOOK FOR THESE OTHER TITLES IN THE VOGUE KNITTING ON THE GO! SERIES...

■

BABY BLANKETS	KIDS KNITS
BABY BLANKETS TWO	KIDS KNITS TWO
BABY GIFTS	MITTENS & GLOVES
BABY KNITS	PILLOWS
BAGS & BACKPACKS	PONCHOS
BEGINNER BASICS	SCARVES
CAPS & HATS	SCARVES TWO
CAPS & HATS TWO	SHAWLS
CHUNKY KNITS	SOCKS
CHUNKY SCARVES & HATS	SOCKS TWO
CROCHETED BAGS	TEEN KNITS
CROCHET BASICS	TODDLER KNITS
CROCHETED HATS	VINTAGE KNITS
FELTING	WEEKEND KNITS